Ta-Dah
Scissor Sisters

© 2006 by International Music Publications Ltd
First published by International Music Publications Ltd in 2006
International Music Publications Ltd is a Faber Music company
3 Queen Square, London WC1N 3AU

Arranged by Cat Hopkins
Engraved by Camden Music
Edited by Lucy Holliday

Photography by Rocky Schenck
Original Art Direction by Cally at Antar
Faber Artwork by Lydia Merrills-Ashcroft

Printed in England by Caligraving Ltd
All rights reserved

ISBN10: 0-571-52763-9
ISBN13: 978-0-571-52763-2

To buy Faber Music publications or to find out about
the full range of titles available, please contact your
local music retailer or Faber Music sales enquiries:

Faber Music Ltd, Burnt Mill, Elizabeth Way, Harlow,
CM20 2HX England

Tel: +44(0)1279 82 89 82
Fax: +44(0)1279 82 89 83
sales@fabermusic.com
fabermusic.com

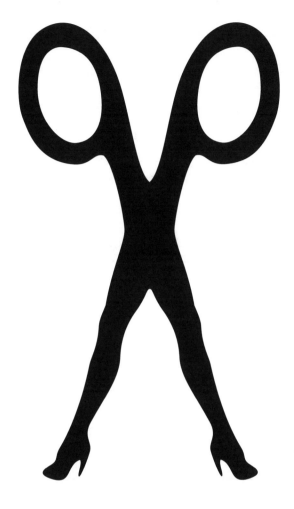

I DON'T FEEL LIKE DANCIN'

Words and Music by Scott Hoffman, Jason Sellards and Elton John

You____ can't make me dance___

SHE'S MY MAN

Words and Music by Scott Hoffman and Jason Sellards

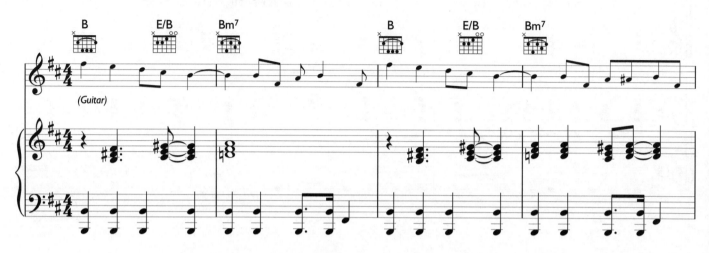

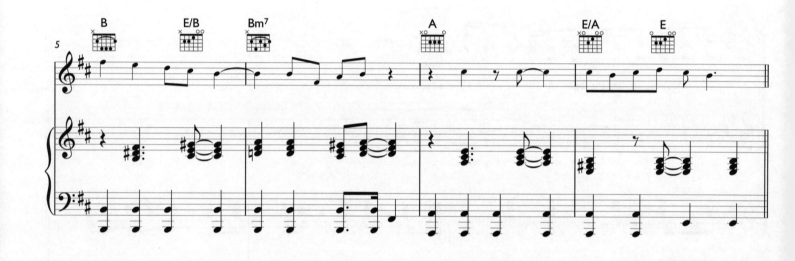

I CAN'T DECIDE

Words and Music by Scott Hoffman and Jason Sellards

Lock the doors___ and close the blinds, we're go-ing for a ride.___

LIGHTS

Words and Music by Scott Hoffman, Jason Sellards and Carlos Alomar

ma-ma told me one____ thing I'll re-mem-ber till____ I die:____ the one you want the most____ will be____ the one

____ that you__ de-fy.____ The times they're gon - na love you, it's like stich-es in__ the scar.__ You can ne -

34

LAND OF A THOUSAND WORDS

Words and Music by Scott Hoffman and Jason Sellards

INTERMISSION

Words and Music by Scott Hoffman, Jason Sellards and Elton John

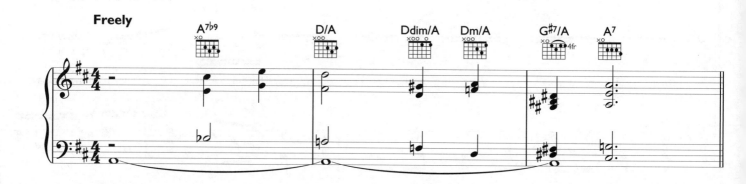

1. When you're stand-ing on the side of a hill,___ feel-ing like your day may be done,___
2. Some-times___ you're filled___ with the no-tion the af-ter-life's a mo-ment a-way,___

___ here it comes;___ the straw-ber-ry smog,___
___ you want to tell some-one the way that you feel___ but

42

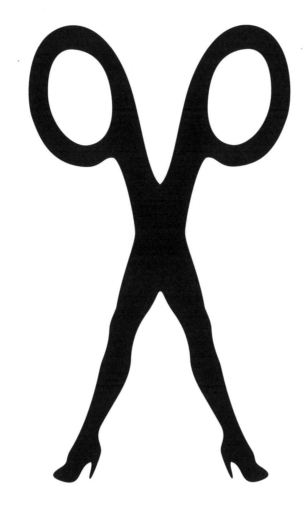

KISS YOU OFF

Words and Music by Scott Hoffman, Jason Sellards and Ana Lynch

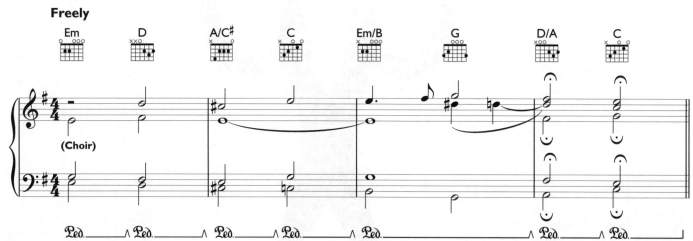

Kiss you off my lips, I don't need an-oth-er tube of that dime store lip - stick. Well, I

think I'm gon-na buy me a brand new shade of man.

D.§ al Coda

OOH

Words and Music by Scott Hoffman, Jason Sellards and Derek Gruen

PAUL McCARTNEY

Words and Music by Scott Hoffman, Jason Sellards,
Derek Gruen and Carlos Alomar

(Guitar Solo)

in love with your sound.

D.𝄋 al Coda

Is it the

Coda

Ah,_____ your song, it gets me by. By,___

(BV 2° only)

_____ say by,_____ when you're sing-ing I'll be with you 'til the ex-it line. (Saxophone solo 2° only)

THE OTHER SIDE

Words and Music by Scott Hoffman, Jason Sellards and John Garden

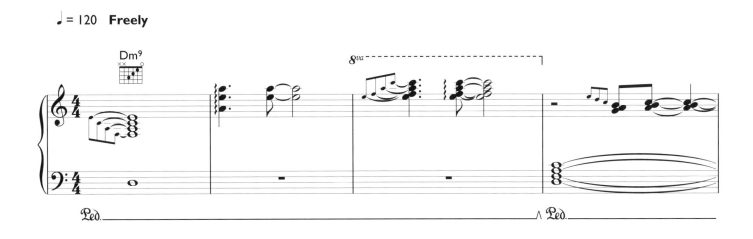

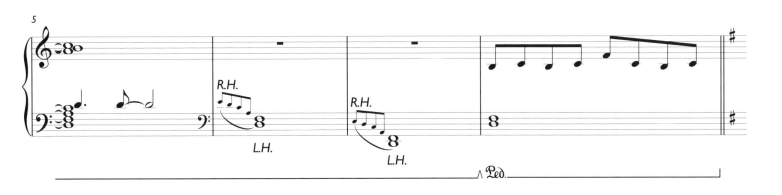

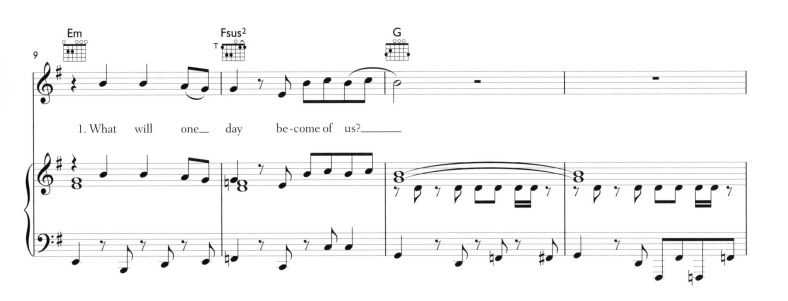

1. What will one day be-come of us?

We'll grow as grass un - der__ their feet.__

No - one__ here will ev - er know your name,__

and you still lie here next to me.__

MIGHT TELL YOU TONIGHT

Words and Music by Scott Hoffman and Jason Sellards

EVERYBODY WANTS THE SAME THING

Words and Music by Scott Hoffman, Jason Sellards,
Ana Lynch, Patrick Seacor and Paul Leschen

(Gtr. solo)

Play 4 times ad lib., one BV entering on each repeat

What is it that you want? What is it that you give?_ Where

right here's where I'm find-ing it,____ that's how I'm gon-na live.____

(How am I gon-na live?__ How am I gon-na live?__

How am I gon-na live?__ How am I gon-na live?)__

Come on, come on, come on, come on, come on, come on, come on, come on.

TRANSISTOR

Words and Music by Scott Hoffman and Jason Sellards

-sis - tor, let the new world_ hit you, and help_

_ me { reach_ / find_ } the stars_ be - tween your eyes.___ (Like to love...) Tran-

(Sing 2° only)

To Coda ⊕

-sis - tor.

N.C. (G)